2014 NOVEMBER NOVEMBRE | NOVIEMBRE

SUN dim | dom	MON lun | lun	TUE mar | mar	WED mer | miér	THU jeu | jue	FRI ven | vier	SAT sam | sáb
26	27	28	29	30	31	1
2	3	4	5	6	7	8
9	10	11	12	13	14	15
16	17	18	19	20	21	22
23 / 30	24	25	26	27	28	29

2014 DECEMBER DÉCEMBRE | DICIEMBRE

SUN dim | dom	MON lun | lun	TUE mar | mar	WED mer | miér	THU jeu | jue	FRI ven | vier	SAT sam | sáb
30	1	2	3	4	5	6
7	8	9	10	11	12	13
14	15	16	17	18	19	20
21	22	23	24	25	26	27
28	29	30	31	1	2	3

All times shown are in Universal Time (UT), which approximates Greenwich Mean Time (GMT). Adjusting the UT to the reader's time zone may change the calendar dates of certain lunar events. Events can differ from dates shown due to regional or sectarian observances. Publisher shall not be responsible or liable for any reliance on the displayed event dates. For additional calendar events, visit browntrout.com. No portion of this calendar may be _____ digitized, or copied in any form without prior written permission fro _____

BrownTrout Offices

USA–World Headquarters
BrownTrout Publishers, Inc.
201 Continental Blvd., Suite 200
El Segundo, CA 90245 USA
(1) 310 607 9010
Toll Free: 800 777 7812
sales@browntrout.com

Canada
BrownTrout Publishers, Ltd.
55 Cork Street East, Suite 307
Guelph ON N1H 2W7, Canada
(1) 519 821 8882
Canada Toll Free: 1 888 254 5842
sales@browntrout.ca

Mexico
Editorial SalmoTruti, SA de CV
Hegel 153 Int. 903, Colonia Polanco
Del. Miguel Hidalgo, 11560 Mexico D.F.
Mexico
(52-55) 5545 0492
Mexico Toll Free: 01 800 716 7420
ventas@salmotruti.com.mx

United Kingdom
BrownTrout Publishers Ltd.
Redland Office Centre, 157 Redland Rd.
Bristol, BS6 6YE, United Kingdom
(44) 117 317 1880
UK Freephone: 0800 169 3718
sales@browntroutuk.com

Australia and New Zealand
BrownTrout Publishers Pty. Ltd.
477 Lygon Street
Brunswick East VIC 3057, Australia
(61) 3 9384 7100
Australia Toll Free: 1 800 111 882
New Zealand Toll Free: 0 800 888 112
sales@browntrout.com.au

Connecting People to Their Passions

 browntrout.com
facebook.com/browntroutpublishers
pinterest.com/browntroutpub
@browntroutpub

BrownTrout Earth Friendly

E _____
_____
for _____
soy- an _____
which are less harmfu _____
petroleum-based alte _____
a digital workflow to re _____
recycle all overstock or _____

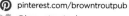

2015

JANUARY

JANVIER | ENERO

DECEMBER 2014
	1	2	3	4	5	6
7	8	9	10	11	12	13
14	15	16	17	18	19	20
21	22	23	24	25	26	27
28	29	30	31			

FEBRUARY 2015
1	2	3	4	5	6	7
8	9	10	11	12	13	14
15	16	17	18	19	20	21
22	23	24	25	26	27	28

SUNDAY dim | dom	MONDAY lun | lun	TUESDAY mar | mar	WEDNESDAY mer | miér	THURSDAY jeu | jue	FRIDAY ven | vier	SATURDAY sam | sáb
28	29	30	31	1 New Year's Day	2 Day after New Year's Day (NZ; SCT)	3
4 Full Moon 4:53 U.T.	5	6	7	8	9	10
11	12	13 Epiphany Last Quarter 9:46 U.T.	14	15	16	17
18	19	20 New Moon 13:14 U.T.	21	22	23	24
25 Burns Night (SCT)	26 Martin Luther King Jr. Day (US) Australia Day (AU)	27 First Quarter 4:48 U.T. International Holocaust Remembrance Day (UN)	28	29	30	31

Wolf Cubs

JANUARY 2015						
				1	2	3
4	5	6	7	8	9	10
11	12	13	14	15	16	17
18	19	20	21	22	23	24
25	26	27	28	29	30	31

MARCH 2015						
1	2	3	4	5	6	7
8	9	10	11	12	13	14
15	16	17	18	19	20	21
22	23	24	25	26	27	28
29	30	31				

SUNDAY dim | dom	MONDAY lun | lun	TUESDAY mar | mar	WEDNESDAY mer | miér	THURSDAY jeu | jue	FRIDAY ven | vier	SATURDAY sam | sáb
1	**2** Groundhog Day Día de la Candelaria (MX)	**3** Full Moon 23:09 U.T.	**4**	**5** Día de la Constitución (MX)	**6** Waitangi Day (NZ)	**7**
8	**9** Family Day (BC-CAN)	**10**	**11** Last Quarter 3:50 U.T.	**12** Lincoln's Birthday (US)	**13**	**14** Valentine's Day
15	**16** Presidents' Day (US) Family Day (AB/ON/SK-CAN) Louis Riel Day (MB-CAN)	**17** New Moon 23:47 U.T. Shrove Tuesday Mardi Gras	**18** Ash Wednesday	**19** Chinese New Year (Sheep)	**20**	**21**
22 Washington's Birthday (US)	**23** Great Lent begins (Orthodox)	**24** First Quarter 17:14 U.T. Día de la Bandera (MX)	**25**	**26**	**27**	**28**
1	2	3	4	5	6	7

Wolf Cubs

FEBRUARY 2015

1	2	3	4	5	6	7
8	9	10	11	12	13	14
15	16	17	18	19	20	21
22	23	24	25	26	27	28

APRIL 2015

		1	2	3	4
5	6	7	8	9	10	11
12	13	14	15	16	17	18
19	20	21	22	23	24	25
26	27	28	29	30		

SUNDAY dim | dom	MONDAY lun | lun	TUESDAY mar | mar	WEDNESDAY mer | miér	THURSDAY jeu | jue	FRIDAY ven | vier	SATURDAY sam | sáb
1 St. David's Day (WAL)	**2** Labour Day (WA-AU)	**3**	**4** Full Moon 18:05 U.T. ○	**5**	**6**	**7**
8 International Women's Day Daylight Saving Time begins (US; CAN)	**9** Canberra Day (ACT-AU) Labour Day (VIC-AU) Eight Hours Day (TAS-AU) Adelaide Cup (SA-AU) Commonwealth Day	**10**	**11** Purim begins at sundown	**12**	**13** Last Quarter 17:48 U.T. ◑	**14**
15 Mothering Sunday (UK)	**16**	**17** St. Patrick's Day	**18**	**19**	**20** Spring begins New Moon 9:36 U.T. ●	**21** Natalicio de Benito Juárez (MX)
22	**23**	**24**	**25**	**26** First Quarter 7:43 U.T. ◑	**27**	**28**
29 Palm Sunday European Summer Time begins	**30**	**31**	1	2	3	4

Wolf Cubs

2015 APRIL
AVRIL | ABRIL

MARCH 2015

1	2	3	4	5	6	7
8	9	10	11	12	13	14
15	16	17	18	19	20	21
22	23	24	25	26	27	28
29	30	31				

MAY 2015

					1	2
3	4	5	6	7	8	9
10	11	12	13	14	15	16
17	18	19	20	21	22	23
24	25	26	27	28	29	30
31						

SUNDAY dim | dom	MONDAY lun | lun	TUESDAY mar | mar	WEDNESDAY mer | miér	THURSDAY jeu | jue	FRIDAY ven | vier	SATURDAY sam | sáb
29	30	31	**1** April Fools' Day	**2** Maundy Thursday	**3** Good Friday, Bank Holiday (UK), Passover begins at sundown	**4** Full Moon 12:05 U.T.
5 Easter Sunday, Daylight Saving Time ends (AU; NZ)	**6** Easter Monday, Bank Holiday (UK except SCT; IRL)	**7**	**8**	**9**	**10**	**11** Holy Saturday
12 Last Quarter 3:44 U.T., Pascha (Orthodox)	**13**	**14**	**15**	**16**	**17** New Moon 18:57 U.T.	**18**
19	**20**	**21**	**22** Yom Hashoah begins at sundown, Earth Day, Administrative Professionals Day	**23** St. George's Day (ENG)	**24** First Quarter 23:55 U.T., Arbor Day (US)	**25** ANZAC Day (AU; NZ)
26	**27** Koningsdag (NL)	**28** Birthday of Queen Elizabeth II	**29**	**30** Día del Niño (MX)	1	2

Wolf Cubs

APRIL 2015

		1	2	3	4
5	6	7	8	9	10	11
12	13	14	15	16	17	18
19	20	21	22	23	24	25
26	27	28	29	30		

JUNE 2015

	1	2	3	4	5	6
7	8	9	10	11	12	13
14	15	16	17	18	19	20
21	22	23	24	25	26	27
28	29	30				

SUNDAY dim | dom	MONDAY lun | lun	TUESDAY mar | mar	WEDNESDAY mer | miér	THURSDAY jeu | jue	FRIDAY ven | vier	SATURDAY sam | sáb
26	27	28	29	30	1 — May Day; International Workers' Day; Labor Day (MX); Dag van de Arbeid (BE; NL)	2
3 — National Pet Week (US)	4 — Full Moon 3:42 U.T.; May Day (NT–AU); Bank Holiday (UK; IRL); Dodenherdenking (NL)	5 — Cinco de Mayo; Batalla de Puebla (MX); Bevrijdingsdag (NL)	6	7 — National Day of Prayer (US)	8 — Fête de la Victoire (FR)	9
10 — Mother's Day (US; AU; BE; CAN; NL; NZ); Día de las Madres (MX)	11 — Last Quarter 10:36 U.T.	12	13	14 — Ascension	15 — Día del Maestro (MX)	16 — Armed Forces Day (US)
17	18 — New Moon 4:13 U.T.; Victoria Day/Fête de la Reine (CAN); Journée nationale des patriotes/ National Patriots' Day (QC–CAN)	19	20	21	22	23
24 — Pentecost (Whitsun)	25 — First Quarter 17:19 U.T.; Memorial Day (US); Spring Bank Holiday (UK); Pentecost Monday	26	27	28	29	30
31 — Fête des Mères (FR)						

Wolf Cubs

2015 JUNE

JUIN | JUNIO

MAY 2015

					1	2
3	4	5	6	7	8	9
10	11	12	13	14	15	16
17	18	19	20	21	22	23
24	25	26	27	28	29	30
31						

JULY 2015

			1	2	3	4
5	6	7	8	9	10	11
12	13	14	15	16	17	18
19	20	21	22	23	24	25
26	27	28	29	30	31	

SUNDAY dim | dom	MONDAY lun | lun	TUESDAY mar | mar	WEDNESDAY mer | miér	THURSDAY jeu | jue	FRIDAY ven | vier	SATURDAY sam | sáb
31	**1**	Full Moon 16:19 U.T. ○ **2**	**3**	**4**	**5**	**6**
7	Public Holiday (IRL) Queen's Birthday (NZ) Western Australia Day (WA–AU) **8**	Last Quarter 15:42 U.T. ◐ **9**	**10**	**11**	**12**	**13**
14	Queen's Birthday (AU except WA) **15**	New Moon 14:05 U.T. ● **16**	**17**	**18**	**19**	Queen's Official Birthday (tentative) (UK) **20**
Flag Day (US) Vaderdag/Fête des Pères (BE) *Summer begins* **21**	**22**	**23**	Ramadan begins at sundown First Quarter 11:02 U.T. ◑ **24**	**25**	**26**	**27**
Father's Day (US; CAN; NL; UK, MX) National Aboriginal Day/Journée nationale des Autochtones (CAN) **28**	Discovery Day (NL–CAN) **29**	**30**	Fête nationale du Québec/ Saint-Jean-Baptiste Day (QC–CAN) **1**	**2**	**3**	**4**

Wolf Cubs

2015

JULY

JUILLET | JULIO

JUNE 2015							AUGUST 2015						
	1	2	3	4	5	6							1
7	8	9	10	11	12	13	2	3	4	5	6	7	8
14	15	16	17	18	19	20	9	10	11	12	13	14	15
21	22	23	24	25	26	27	16	17	18	19	20	21	22
28	29	30					23	24	25	26	27	28	29
							30	31					

SUNDAY dim | dom	MONDAY lun | lun	TUESDAY mar | mar	WEDNESDAY mer | miér	THURSDAY jeu | jue	FRIDAY ven | vier	SATURDAY sam | sáb
28	29	30	1	2 Full Moon 2:20 U.T.	3	4
5	6	7	8 Canada Day/Fête du Canada (CAN) Last Quarter 20:24 U.T.	9	10	11 Independence Day (US)
12	13	14	15 Nunavut Day (NU-CAN) New Moon 1:24 U.T.	16	17	18 Feest van de Vlaamse Gemeenschap (BE)
19	20 Bank Holiday (NIR)	21 Fête nationale de la France (FR)	22	23 Eid al-Fitr begins at sundown	24 First Quarter 4:04 U.T.	25
26	27	28 Nationale feestdag/Fête nationale de la Belgique (BE)	29	30	31 Full Moon 10:43 U.T.	1

Wolf Cubs

JULY 2015						
		1	2	3	4	
5	6	7	8	9	10	11
12	13	14	15	16	17	18
19	20	21	22	23	24	25
26	27	28	29	30	31	

SEPTEMBER 2015						
	1	2	3	4	5	
6	7	8	9	10	11	12
13	14	15	16	17	18	19
20	21	22	23	24	25	26
27	28	29	30			

SUNDAY dim | dom	MONDAY lun | lun	TUESDAY mar | mar	WEDNESDAY mer | miér	THURSDAY jeu | jue	FRIDAY ven | vier	SATURDAY sam | sáb
26	27	28	29	30	31	1
2	3	4	5	6 Last Quarter 2:03 U.T.	7	8
9	10 Civic Holiday/Congé civique (CAN) Bank Holiday (NSW-AU; IRL; SCT) Picnic Day (NT-AU)	11	12	13 New Moon 14:53 U.T.	14	15
16	17	18	19	20	21 Assumption First Quarter 19:31 U.T.	22
23	24 Discovery Day (YT-CAN)	25	26	27	28 Full Moon 18:35 U.T.	29
30	31 Summer Bank Holiday (UK except SCT)					

Wolf Cubs

2015 | SEPTEMBER

SEPTEMBRE | SEPTIEMBRE

AUGUST 2015
					1
2	3	4	5	6	7	8
9	10	11	12	13	14	15
16	17	18	19	20	21	22
23	24	25	26	27	28	29
30	31					

OCTOBER 2015
				1	2	3
4	5	6	7	8	9	10
11	12	13	14	15	16	17
18	19	20	21	22	23	24
25	26	27	28	29	30	31

SUNDAY dim | dom	MONDAY lun | lun	TUESDAY mar | mar	WEDNESDAY mer | miér	THURSDAY jeu | jue	FRIDAY ven | vier	SATURDAY sam | sáb
30	31	1	2	3	4	5 Last Quarter 9:54 U.T.
6	7	8	9	10	11	12
13 Father's Day (AU; NZ) New Moon 6:41 U.T.	14 Labor Day (US) Labour Day/Fête du Travail (CAN)	15	16	17	18 Patriot Day/National Day of Service and Remembrance (US)	19
20 National Grandparents Day (US) Rosh Hashanah begins at sundown	21 First Quarter 8:59 U.T.	22 Noche del Grito (MX)	23 Día de la Independencia (MX) Autumn begins	24	25	26
27 Fête de la Communauté française (BE) Daylight Saving Time begins (NZ)	28 UN International Day of Peace Full Moon 2:50 U.T. Queen's Birthday (WA-AU) Family & Community Day (ACT-AU)	29 Yom Kippur begins at sundown Eid al-Adha begins at sundown	30	1	2	3

Wolf Cubs

2015 OCTOBER

OCTOBRE | OCTUBRE

SEPTEMBER 2015

		1	2	3	4	5
6	7	8	9	10	11	12
13	14	15	16	17	18	19
20	21	22	23	24	25	26
27	28	29	30			

NOVEMBER 2015

1	2	3	4	5	6	7
8	9	10	11	12	13	14
15	16	17	18	19	20	21
22	23	24	25	26	27	28
29	30					

SUNDAY dim | dom	MONDAY lun | lun	TUESDAY mar | mar	WEDNESDAY mer | miér	THURSDAY jeu | jue	FRIDAY ven | vier	SATURDAY sam | sáb
27	28	29	30	1	2	3
Last Quarter 21:06 U.T. ◑ **4** World Animal Day Daylight Saving Time begins (AU except WA/QLD/NT)	5 Labour Day (ACT/NSW/QLD/SA–AU)	6	7	8	9	10
11	12 Columbus Day (US) Thanksgiving Day/ Action de grâce (CAN) Día de la Raza (MX)	New Moon 0:06 U.T. ● **13** Muharram begins at sundown	14	15	16 Boss's Day	17
18	19	First Quarter 20:31 U.T. ◐ **20**	21	22 Ashura begins at sundown	23	24 United Nations Day
25 European Summer Time ends	26 Labour Day (NZ) Public Holiday (IRL)	Full Moon 12:05 U.T. ○ **27**	28	29	30	31 Halloween

Wolf Cubs

OCTOBER 2015
					1	2	3
4	5	6	7	8	9	10
11	12	13	14	15	16	17
18	19	20	21	22	23	24
25	26	27	28	29	30	31

DECEMBER 2015
		1	2	3	4	5
6	7	8	9	10	11	12
13	14	15	16	17	18	19
20	21	22	23	24	25	26
27	28	29	30	31		

SUNDAY dim | dom	MONDAY lun | lun	TUESDAY mar | mar	WEDNESDAY mer | miér	THURSDAY jeu | jue	FRIDAY ven | vier	SATURDAY sam | sáb
1	2	Last Quarter 12:24 U.T. 3	4	5	6	7
All Saints' Day Daylight Saving Time ends (US; CAN) 8	All Souls' Day Día de los Muertos (MX) 9	Election Day (US) Melbourne Cup (VIC-AU) 10	New Moon 17:47 U.T. 11	Guy Fawkes Day/Bonfire Night (UK) 12	13	14
Remembrance Sunday (UK) 15	16	17	Veterans' Day (US) Remembrance Day/Jour du Souvenir (AU; CAN) Armistice (BE; FR) 18	First Quarter 6:27 U.T. 19	20	21
Koningsdag/Fête du Roi (BE) 22	23	Full Moon 22:44 U.T. 24	25	26	Día de la Revolución Mexicana (MX) 27	28
Advent 29	St. Andrew's Day (SCT) 30	1	2	Thanksgiving Day (US) 3	4	5

Wolf Cubs